# READY TO LE...

# Pre-Kindergarten

# Reading
## Workbook

## Table of Contents

# Pre-K Reading Readiness

Parents and caregivers play a critical role in preparing young children for school. Creating a literacy-rich environment with numerous books and opportunities to share reading and writing with your child is essential. This book will help your child through several important building blocks of learning to read, including sounds, print awareness, letters, and more.

Point to the words as you read aloud to your child. This helps them with one-on-one correlation as he or she listens.

## A and B

Trace the uppercase letters with your finger. Then read the sentences below to say the sounds they make.

A is for apple. Apple, apple, a-a-a. What other words start with the A sound?

B is for bear. Bear, bear, b-b-b. What other words start with the B sound?

Trace the uppercase letter C with your finger. Then color the letter.

Find and circle each uppercase C below.

S E C Z

F C B O

B G R C

Trace the uppercase letter D with your finger. Then color the letter.

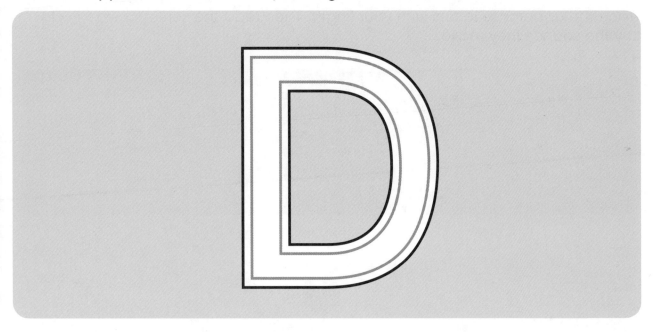

Find and circle each uppercase D below.

C and D

Trace the uppercase letters with your finger. Then read the sentences below to say the sounds they make.

C is for cat. Cat, cat, c-c-c.
What other words start with the C sound?

D is for dog. Dog, dog, d-d-d.
What other words start with the D sound?

Trace the uppercase letter E with your finger. Then color the letter.

Find and circle each uppercase E below.

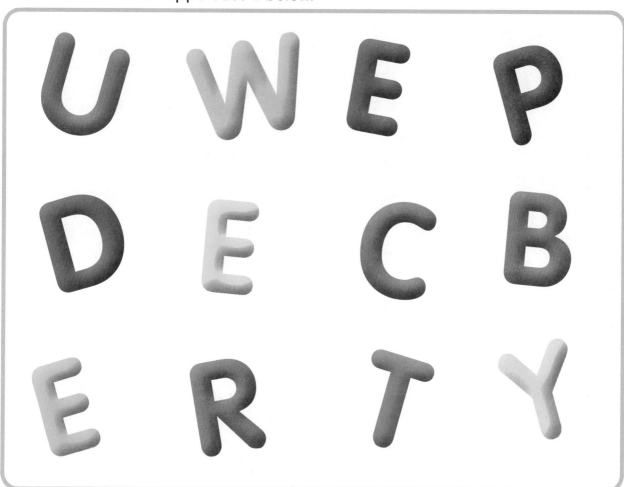

Trace the uppercase letter F with your finger. Then color the letter.

Find and circle each uppercase F below.

E and F

Trace the uppercase letters with your finger. Then read the sentences below to say the sounds they make.

E is for elbow. Elbow, elbow, e-e-e.
What other words start with the E sound?

F is for frog. Frog, frog, f-f-f.
What other words start with the F sound?

Trace the uppercase letter G with your finger. Then color the letter.

Find and circle each uppercase G below.

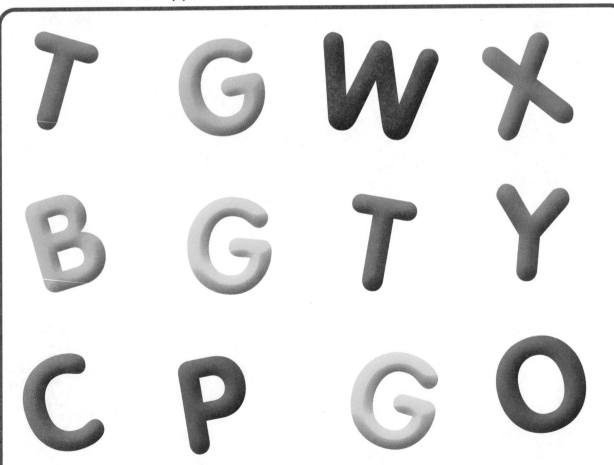

# Letter Names

Trace the uppercase letter H with your finger. Then color the letter.

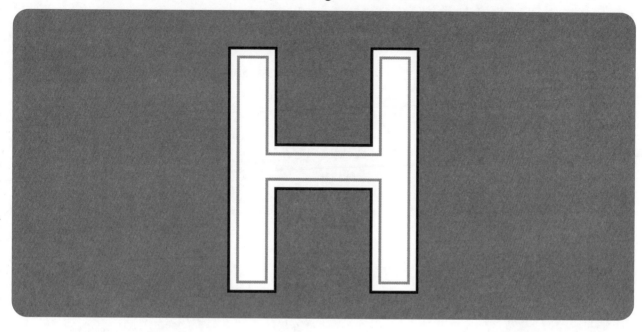

Find and circle each uppercase H below.

G and H

Trace the uppercase letters with your finger. Then read the sentences below to say the sounds they make.

G is for grapes. Grapes, grapes, g-g-g. What other words start with the G sound?

H is for horse. Horse, horse, h-h-h. What other words start with the H sound?

Trace the uppercase letter I with your finger. Then color the letter.

Find and circle each uppercase I below.

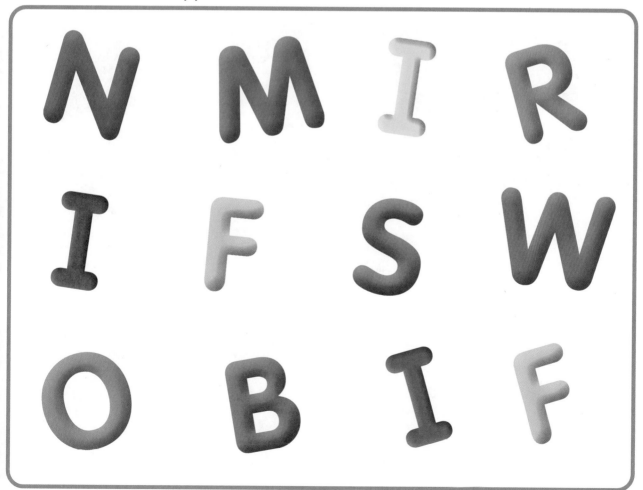

Trace the uppercase letter J with your finger. Then color the letter.

Find and circle each uppercase J below.

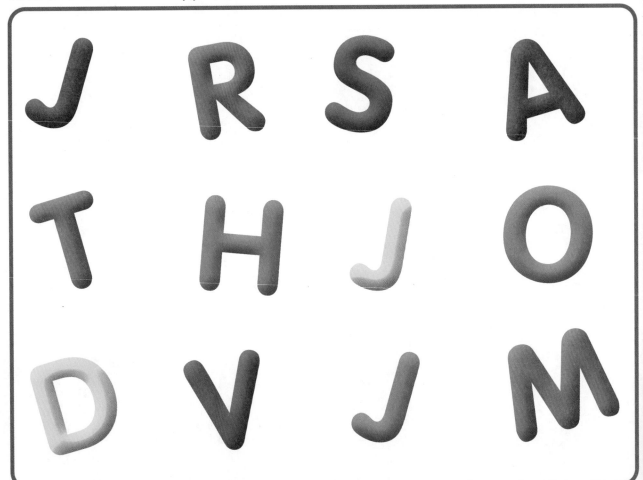

I and J

Trace the uppercase letters with your finger. Then read the sentences below to say the sounds they make.

I is for island. Island, island, i-i-i.
What other words start with the I sound?

J is for jumping. Jumping, jumping, j-j-j.
What other words start with the J sound?

Trace the uppercase letter K with your finger. Then color the letter.

Find and circle each uppercase K below.

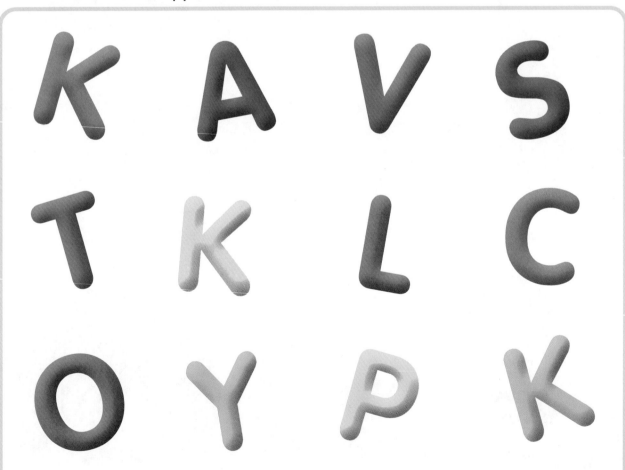

Trace the uppercase letter L with your finger. Then color the letter.

Find and circle each uppercase L below.

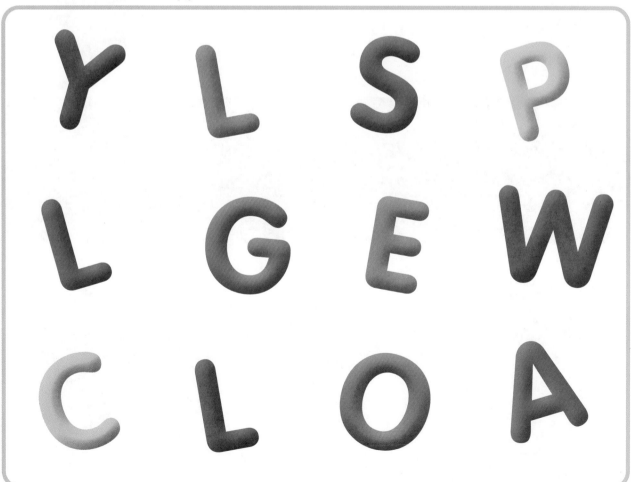

K and L

Trace the uppercase letters with your finger. Then read the sentences below to say the sounds they make.

K is for kangaroo. Kangaroo, kangaroo, k-k-k. What other words start with the K sound?

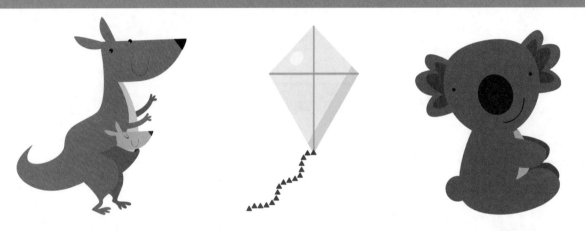

L is for lion. Lion, lion, l-l-l. What other words start with the L sound?

Trace the uppercase letter M with your finger. Then color the letter.

Find and circle each uppercase M below.

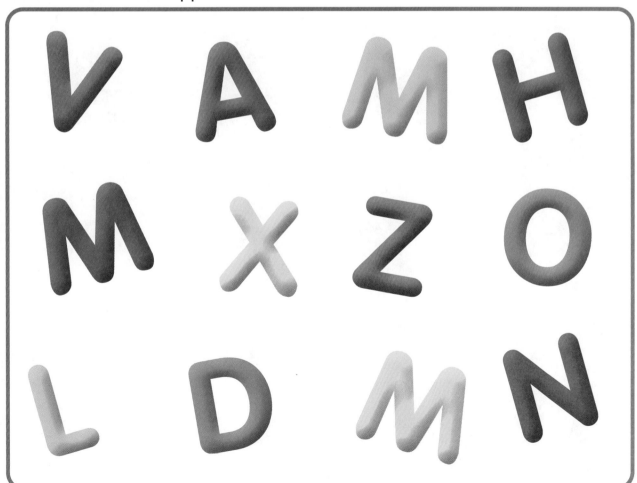

# Letter Names

Trace the uppercase letter N with your finger. Then color the letter.

Find and circle each uppercase N below.

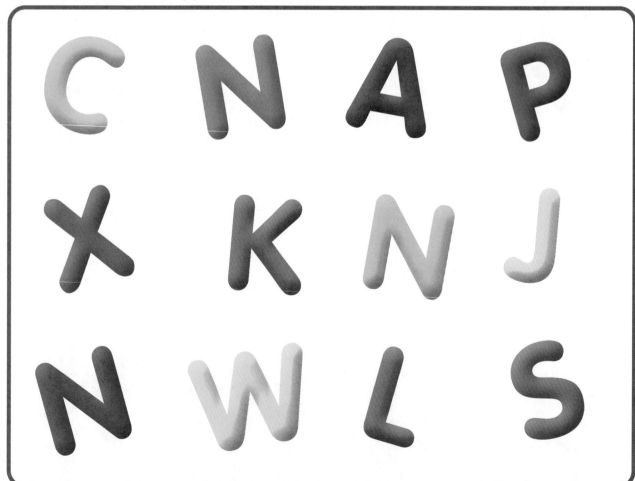

M and N

Trace the uppercase letters with your finger. Then read the sentences below to say the sounds they make.

**M** is for monkey. Monkey, monkey, m-m-m. What other words start with the M sound?

**N** is for necklace. Necklace, necklace, n-n-n. What other words start with the N sound?

Trace the uppercase letter O with your finger. Then color the letter.

Find and circle each uppercase O below.

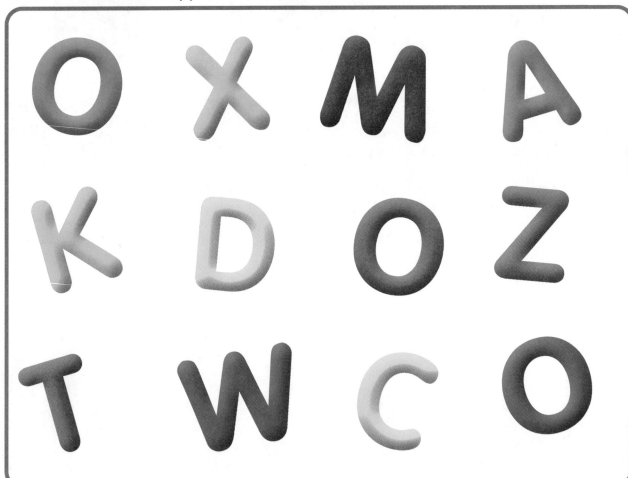

Trace the uppercase letter P with your finger. Then color the letter.

Find and circle each uppercase P below.

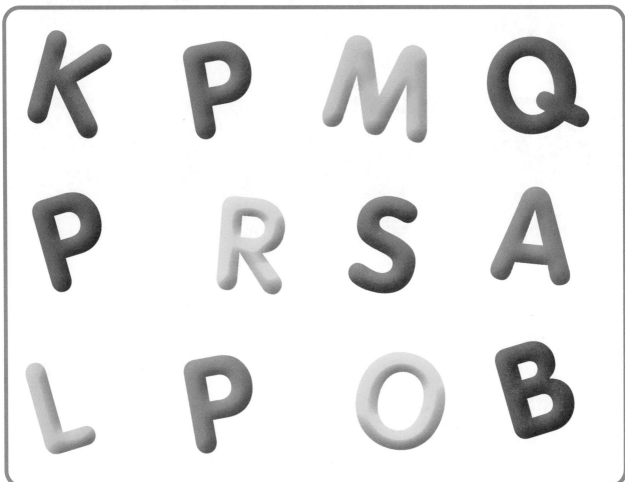

# Letter Sounds

O and P

Trace the uppercase letters with your finger. Then read the sentences below to say the sounds they make.

O is for octopus. Octopus, octopus, o-o-o. What other words start with the O sound?

P is for pencil. Pencil, pencil, p-p-p. What other words start with the P sound?

Trace the uppercase letter Q with your finger. Then color the letter.

Find and circle each uppercase Q below.

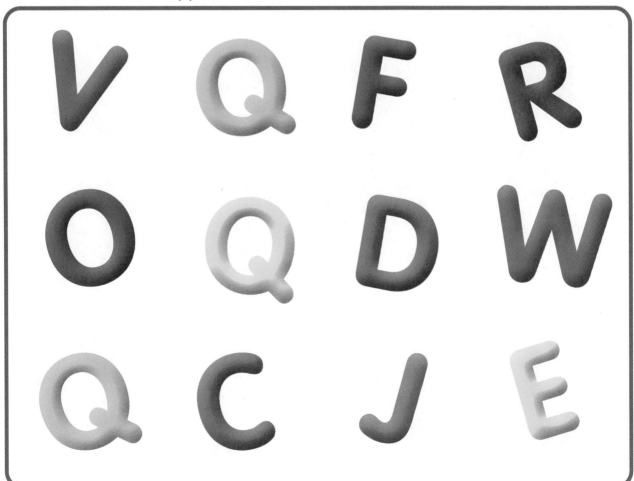

Trace the uppercase letter R with your finger. Then color the letter.

Find and circle each uppercase R below.

## Q and R

Trace the uppercase letters with your finger. Then read the sentences below to say the sounds they make.

Q is for queen. Queen, queen, q-q-q. What other words start with the Q sound?

R is for rabbit. Rabbit, rabbit, r-r-r. What other words start with the R sound?

Trace the uppercase letter S with your finger. Then color the letter.

Find and circle each uppercase S below.

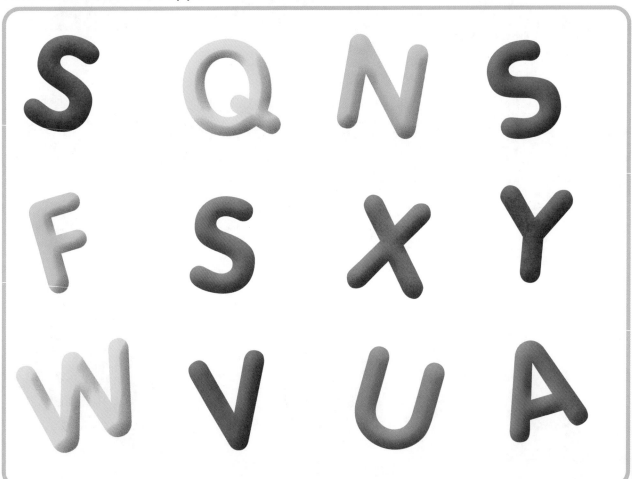

# Letter Names

Trace the uppercase letter T with your finger. Then color the letter.

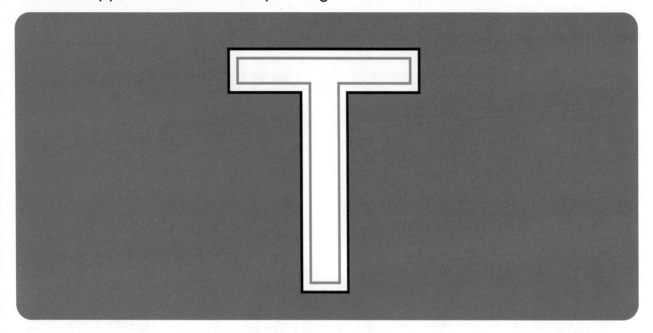

Find and circle each uppercase T below.

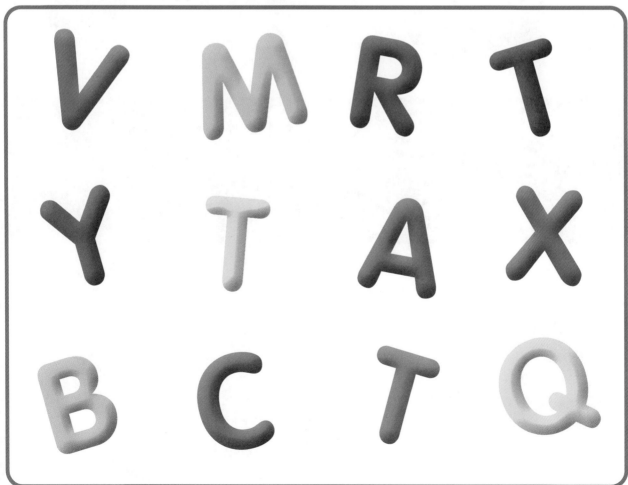

S and T

Trace the uppercase letters with your finger. Then read the sentences below to say the sounds they make.

S is for snake. Snake, snake, s-s-s.
What other words start with the S sound?

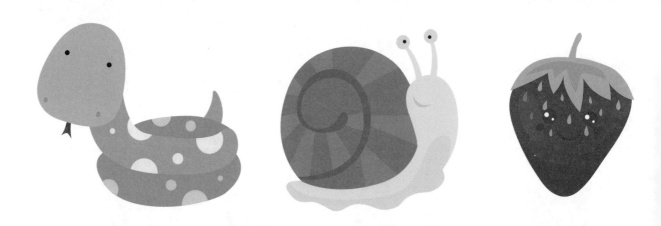

T is for turtle. Turtle, turtle, t-t-t.
What other words start with the T sound?

Trace the uppercase letter U with your finger. Then color the letter.

Find and circle each uppercase U below.

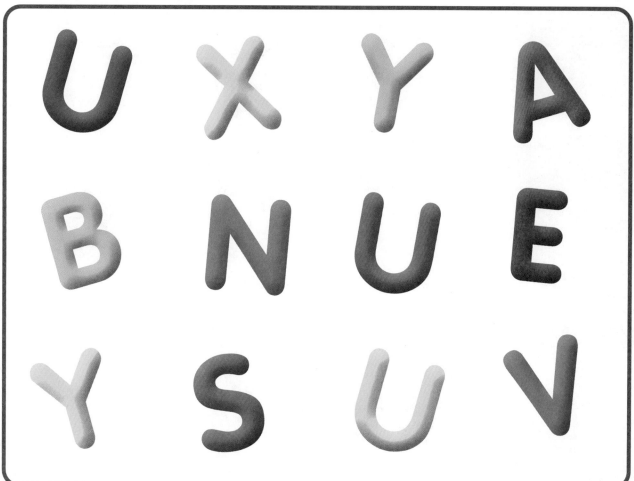

33

Trace the uppercase letter V with your finger. Then color the letter.

Find and circle each uppercase V below.

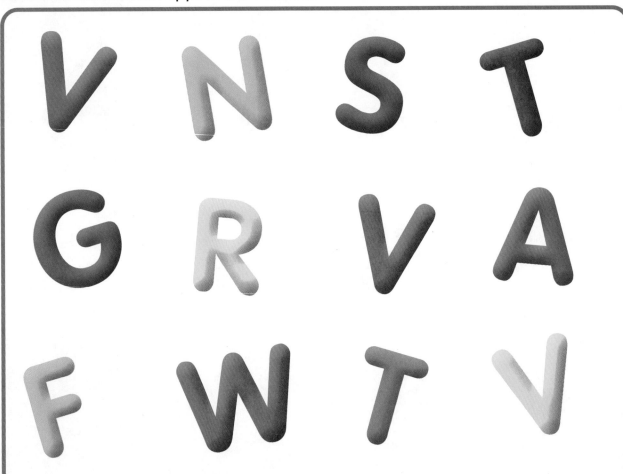

34

U and V

Trace the uppercase letters with your finger. Then read the sentences below to say the sounds they make.

U is for ukulele. Ukulele, ukulele, u-u-u. What other words start with the U sound?

V is for violin. Violin, violin, v-v-v. What other words start with the V sound?

Trace the uppercase letter W with your finger. Then color the letter.

Find and circle each uppercase W below.

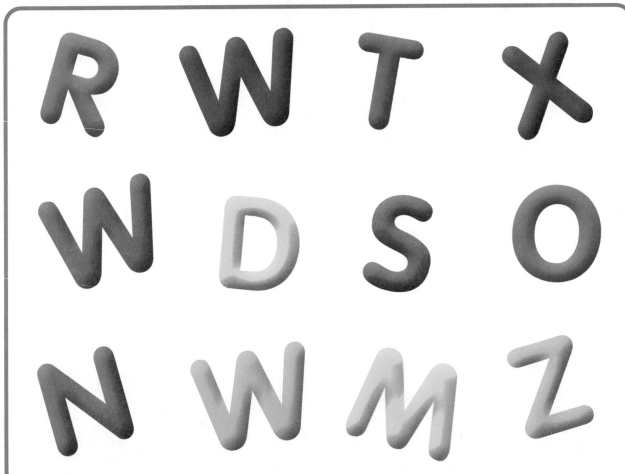

# Letter Names

Trace the uppercase letter X with your finger. Then color the letter.

Find and circle each uppercase X below.

W and X

Trace the uppercase letters with your finger. Then read the sentences below to say the sounds they make.

W is for walrus. Walrus, walrus, w–w–w. What other words start with the W sound?

X is for x-ray. X-ray, x-ray, x–x–x. What other words have an X sound in them?

# Letter Names

Trace the uppercase letter Y with your finger. Then color the letter.

Find and circle each uppercase Y below.

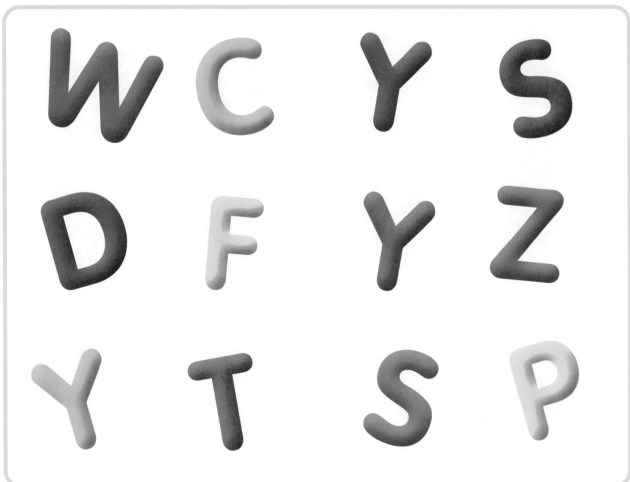

39

Trace the uppercase letter Z with your finger. Then color the letter.

Find and circle each uppercase Z below.

Y and Z

Trace the uppercase letters with your finger. Then read the sentences below to say the sounds they make.

**Y** is for yo-yo. Yo-yo, yo-yo, y-y-y. What other words start with the Y sound?

**Z** is for zebra. Zebra, zebra, z-z-z. What other words start with the Z sound?

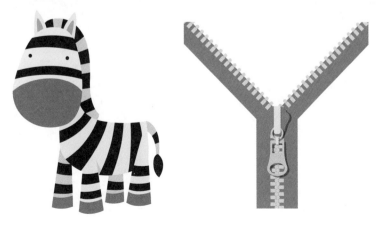

# ABC Order

Sing the ABC song and point to the letters. Write the missing letters on the blank shells.

# ABC Order

Sing the ABC song and point to the letters. Write the missing letters in the blank train cars.

A B _ D E _

G H _ J K

L _ N

O _ Q R _ T

U V W _ Y Z

# ABC Order

Sing the ABC song and point to the letters. Write the missing letters on the blank quilt squares.

# ABC Order

Sing the ABC song and point to the letters. Write the missing letters on the blank books.

# Beginning Sounds

Draw a line from each uppercase letter to the picture that starts with its sound.

# Beginning Sounds

Draw a line from each uppercase letter to the picture that starts with its sound.

# Beginning Sounds

Draw a line from each letter to the picture that starts with its sound.

48

# Beginning Sounds

Draw a line from each letter to the picture that starts with its sound.

 K

 M

 O

 Q

 S

Read the rhyme aloud and listen for the words that sound the same. Circle the rhyming words with your favorite crayon.

"I wish," said the fish,
"I could eat from a dish!"

# Rhyming Poems

Read the rhyme aloud and listen for the words that sound the same. Circle the rhyming words with your favorite crayon.

Little Joan
Sat all alone
Licking away
At her ice-cream cone.

# Rhyming Poems

Read the rhyme aloud and listen for the words that sound the same. Circle the rhyming words with your favorite crayon.

Ding-dong
Rang the gong.
Dinner is ready.
Now come along.

# Rhyming Poems

Read the rhyme aloud and listen for the words that sound the same. Circle the rhyming words with your favorite crayon.

Crunch, crunch,
I love to munch.
A bunch of carrots
To eat for lunch.

What Happens Next?

Look at the pictures below.

Circle the picture that comes next.

What Happens Next?

Look at the pictures below.

Circle the picture that comes next.

What Happens Next?

Look at the pictures below.

Circle the picture that comes next.

# Sequencing

What Happens Next?

Look at the pictures below.

Circle the picture that comes next.

## What Happens Next?
Look at the pictures below.

Circle the picture that comes next.

What Happens Next?

Look at the pictures below.

Circle the picture that comes next.

# ANSWER KEY

### Page 3

### Page 4

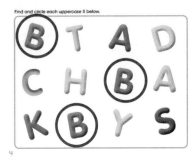

### Page 6

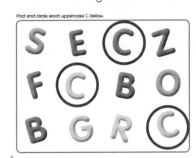

### Page 7

### Page 9

### Page 10

### Page 12

### Page 13

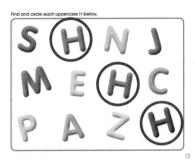

### Page 15

### Page 16

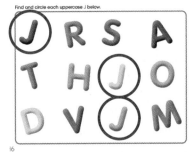

### Page 18

### Page 19

### Page 21

### Page 22

### Page 24

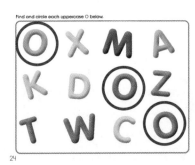

### Page 25

Find and circle each uppercase P below.

### Page 27

Find and circle each uppercase Q below.

### Page 28

Find and circle each uppercase R below.

### Page 30

Find and circle each uppercase S below.

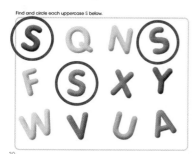

### Page 31

Find and circle each uppercase T below.

### Page 33

Find and circle each uppercase U below.

### Page 34

Find and circle each uppercase V below.

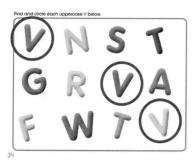

### Page 36

Find and circle each uppercase W below.

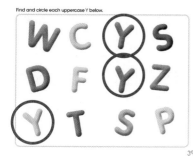

### Page 37

Find and circle each uppercase X below.

### Page 39

Find and circle each uppercase Y below.

### Page 40

Find and circle each uppercase Z below.

### Page 42

**ABC Order**

Sing the ABC song and point to the letters. Write the missing letters on the blank shells.

### Page 43

**ABC Order**

Sing the ABC song and point to the letters. Write the missing letters in the blank train cars.

### Page 44

**ABC Order**

Sing the ABC song and point to the letters. Write the missing letters on the blank quilt squares.

44

### Page 45

**ABC Order**

Sing the ABC song and point to the letters. Write the missing letters on the blank books.

45

### Page 46

**Beginning Sounds**

Draw a line from each uppercase letter to the picture that starts with its sound.

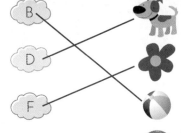

46

### Page 47

**Beginning Sounds**

Draw a line from each uppercase letter to the picture that starts with its sound.

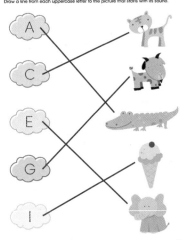

47

### Page 48

**Beginning Sounds**

Draw a line from each letter to the picture that starts with its sound.

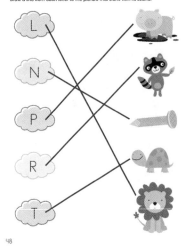

48

### Page 49

**Beginning Sounds**

Draw a line from each letter to the picture that starts with its sound.

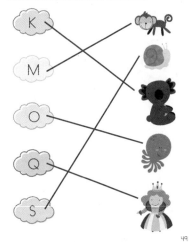

49

### Page 50

**Rhyming Poems**

Read the rhyme aloud and listen for the words that sound the same. Circle the rhyming words with your favorite crayon.

"I wish," said the fish
"I could eat from a dish!"

50

### Page 51

**Rhyming Poems**

Read the rhyme aloud and listen for the words that sound the same. Circle the rhyming words with your favorite crayon.

Little Joan
Sat alone
Licking away
At her ice-cream cone.

51

### Page 52

**Rhyming Poems**

Read the rhyme aloud and listen for the words that sound the same. Circle the rhyming words with your favorite crayon.

Ding dong
Rang the gong
Dinner is ready
Now come along

52

## Page 53

### Rhyming Poems

Read the rhyme aloud and listen for the words that sound the same. Circle the rhyming words with your favorite crayon.

Crunch (crunch)
I love to (munch)
A bunch of carrots
To eat for (lunch)

53

## Page 54

### Sequencing

What Happens Next?
Look at the pictures below.

Circle the picture that comes next.

54

## Page 55

### Sequencing

What Happens Next?
Look at the pictures below.

Circle the picture that comes next.

55

## Page 56

### Sequencing

What Happens Next?
Look at the pictures below.

Circle the picture that comes next.

56

## Page 57

### Sequencing

What Happens Next?
Look at the pictures below.

Circle the picture that comes next.

57

## Page 58

### Sequencing

What Happens Next?
Look at the pictures below.

Circle the picture that comes next.

58

## Page 59

### Sequencing

What Happens Next?
Look at the pictures below.

Circle the picture that comes next.

59

# CERTIFICATE
## of Achievement

has successfully completed
**Pre-K Reading Workbook**

Signed:

Date: